BRIGHT IDEA BOOKS

HOW DO Robots DEFUSE BOMBS?

Yvette LaPierre

raintree

a Capstone company — publishers for children

Raintree is an imprint of Capstone Global Library Limited, a company incorporated in England and Wales having its registered office at 264 Banbury Road, Oxford, OX2 7DY – Registered company number: 6695582

www.raintree.co.uk
myorders@raintree.co.uk

Editor: Megan Gunderson
Designer: Becky Daum
Production Specialist: Colleen McLaren
Originated by Capstone Global Library Limited
Printed and bound in India

ISBN 978 1 4747 7528 1 (hardback)
22 21 20 19 18
10 9 8 7 6 5 4 3 2 1

ISBN 978 1 4747 7352 2 (paperback)
23 22 21 20 19
10 9 8 7 6 5 4 3 2 1

British Library Cataloguing in Publication Data
A full catalogue record for this book is available from the British Library.

Acknowledgements
Alamy: Alain Le Garsmeur "The Troubles" Archive, 17, Open Government License, 18–19, 20; AP Images: Matthias Balk/picture-alliance/dpa, 8–9, 28, Press Association/URN:8519730, 23, Wally Santana, 11; iStockphoto: Caluian, 30–31; Shutterstock Images: ChameleonsEye, 5, Quality Stock Arts, 12–13; US Air Force: Staff Sgt. Manuel J. Martinez, 24–25; US Navy: Mass Communication Specialist 1st Class Peter D. Lawlor, cover, Mass Communication Specialist 2nd Class Derek R. Sanchez, 14–15, Mass Communication Specialist 3rd Class Jumar T. Balacy, 27, Mass Communication Specialist Seaman Charles Oki, 6–7.
Design Elements: iStockphoto, Red Line Editorial, and Shutterstock Images

We would like to thank Aviral Shrivastava, Associate Professor at the School of Computing Informatics and Decision Systems Engineering, Arizona State University for his invaluable help in the preparation of this book. Special thanks also to Lekha Shrivastava for her feedback on this book.

CONTENTS

CHAPTER 1

A ROBOT SAVES
the Day

A soldier is on patrol. He sees a package. It is hidden under a car. It could be a bomb. But it is dangerous to get too close.

The robot rolls on treads like a small tank.

Another soldier stands at a safe distance. She sends in a **remote-controlled** robot.

The robot moves towards the car. It has a camera. This helps the soldier see from far away.

A robot uses special tools to take bombs apart.

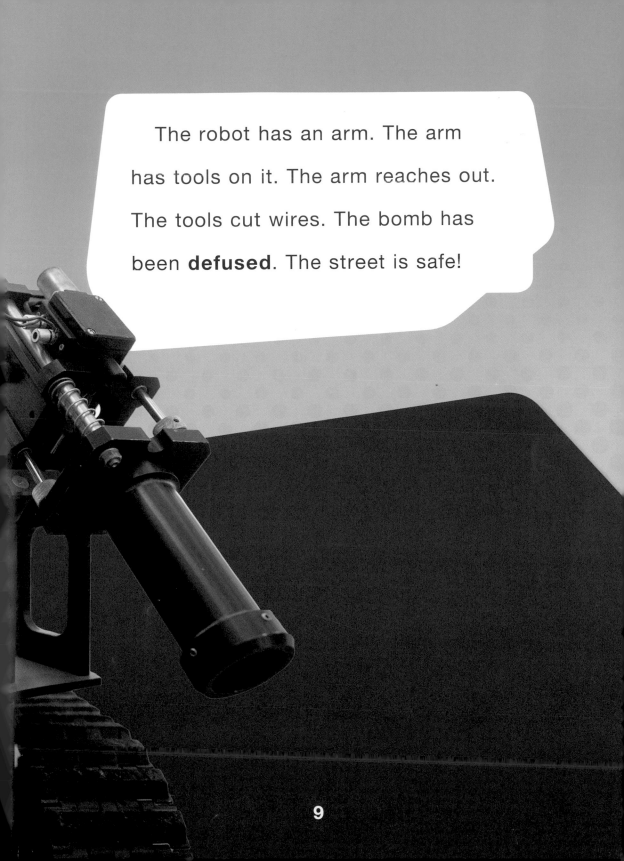

The robot has an arm. The arm has tools on it. The arm reaches out. The tools cut wires. The bomb has been **defused**. The street is safe!

CHAPTER 2

MILITARY
Robots

Robots are machines. Computers control the robots' movements. People write the instructions for the computers.

iRobot is a company that makes bomb-defusing robots. It also makes Roomba, the robot vacuum.

ROBOTS AT WORK

Robots do many jobs. Some explore other planets. Some work in factories. Others clean homes.

The Army uses robots. Robots collect information. They spy. They do dangerous jobs. They keep military soldiers safe.

THE FIRST ROBOTS

The word *robot* was first used in 1921 in a play. It comes from a word meaning "forced labour".

Special suits help protect soldiers from bombs. Using robots is safer.

ROBOTS V. BOMBS

One dangerous job is bomb **disposal**. There are two ways to dispose of a bomb. It can be towed to a safe place and exploded. Or it can be defused.

Soldiers did this job for many years. Many lost their lives. The Army wanted bomb disposal to be safer. Robots were perfect for the job.

THE
Wheelbarrow

The first bomb disposal robot was called the Wheelbarrow. It was made in 1972. It was an electric wheelbarrow. It had a hook on the front. It could hook a bomb and tow it to safety. But the Wheelbarrow had problems.

A soldier controlled the Wheelbarrow with long ropes. The robot could only go the length of the ropes. Sometimes the ropes got tangled.

Robot makers needed to improve the Wheelbarrow.

Engineers found a solution. They added computers. Now soldiers control the robots without ropes or wires. They use **joysticks**, like a computer game.

A modern Wheelbarrow can destroy suspected bombs.

MORE PROBLEMS SOLVED

The soldier could now stand far away. But he needed to see the bomb. Engineers put cameras on the robot. The soldier watches through a monitor. He can see what the robot is doing.

A Wheelbarrow's arm can remove a bomb from under a car.

Early robots had trouble on uneven ground. They tipped over. Engineers replaced the wheels with treads. Treads roll over rocky ground. They even climb stairs.

The Wheelbarrow could tow a bomb away. It could not defuse a bomb. Then engineers added an arm. It had a hand and its joints moved. The hand had tools to take bombs apart.

POLICE ROBOTS

Police also use robots to dispose of bombs.

CHAPTER 4

BOMB DISPOSAL
Robots Today

Today's robots carry many tools. They can go almost anywhere. They come in many sizes.

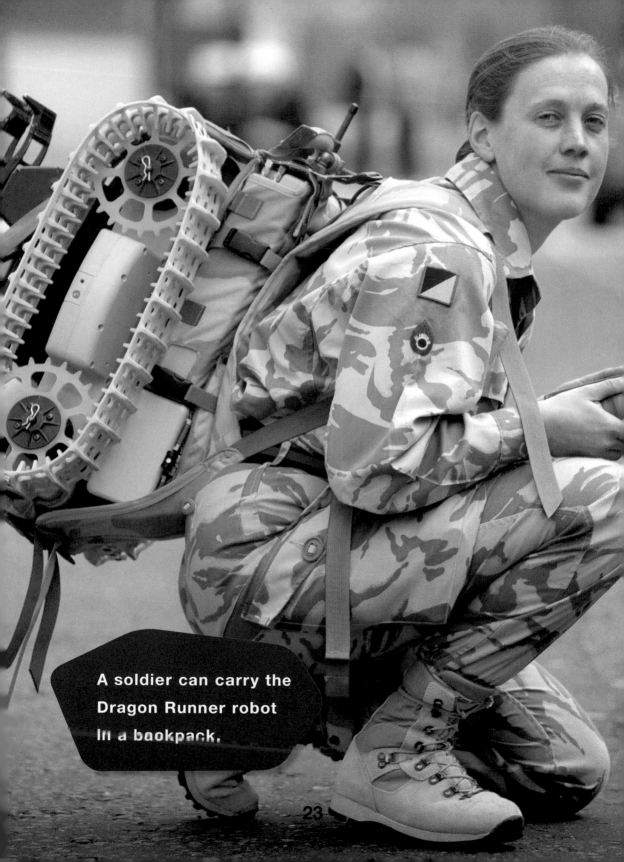

A soldier can carry the Dragon Runner robot in a backpack.

23

Soldiers practise controlling a PackBot.

SMALL BOTS

Soldiers find bombs in tight places.

The iRobot company made the PackBot.

The PackBot can fit in a backpack. Soldiers can roll it under cars. They throw it through windows. It can turn itself over if it lands on its back.

ROBOT SUPERPOWERS

Some robots use X-ray vision to find bombs.

BIG BOTS

Some bomb disposal robots are big. They are the size of bulldozers! They roll on treads. They have a big arm. They clear large fields of **mines** and bombs.

SEA BOTS

Sometimes bombs are underwater. Some robots work in shallow water. The navy uses robot subs. They hunt for mines in the ocean.

Robots go into dangerous places. They get rid of bombs safely. These robots are saving lives.

The US Navy uses robots to clear underwater bombs.

GLOSSARY

defuse
to take apart a bomb before it explodes

disposal
the act of getting rid of or turning into rubbish

engineer
a person who designs machines or structures

joystick
a control stick

mine
an explosive device

remote-controlled
operated from a distance

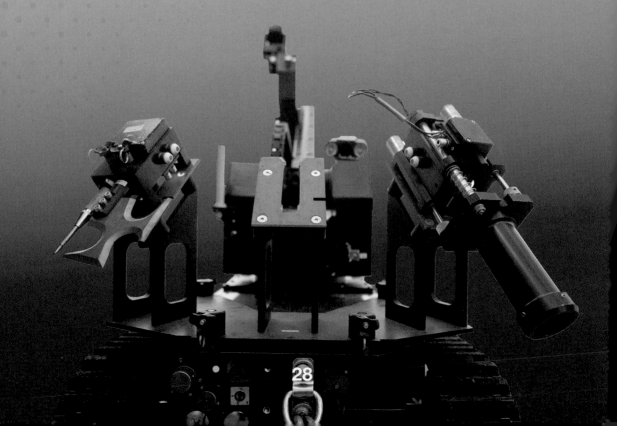

TRIVIA

1. Soldiers use the Talon robot to search for bombs. Police officers use this robot too. It can have up to seven cameras. One camera is for night vision.

2. The US Navy trains dolphins and sea lions to look for mines in the ocean. Robots may soon replace the animals.

3. The Royal Air Force uses robots that fly too. These robots spy on enemies from the air. They are called drones.

4. In the future, robots might work in teams. One can find the bomb. The other can defuse it.

ACTIVITY

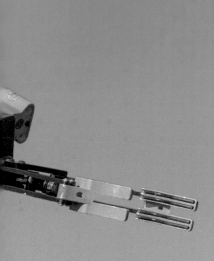

YouTube has lots of videos of bomb-defusing robots at work. Ask an adult to help you find a robot video. It should feature a robot that is not in this book, such as Robo Sally or RE2. Watch a mission from start to finish. Then write your own description of the robot. How is it similar to robots in this book? How is it different?

Military robots can do lots of things. But they aren't perfect. What improvements would you make? What else could robots do for soldiers?

FIND OUT MORE

Books

Building Robots: Robotic Engineers, Daniel R. Faust (PowerKids Press, 2016)

Incredible Robots in the Armed Forces, Louise and Richard Spilsbury (Raintree, 2018)

Military Drones, Matt Chandler (Raintree, 2018)

Military Robots (Robot Innovations series), Brett S. Martin (North Star Classroom, 2018)

Websites

Robots on Explain That Stuff!:
www.explainthatstuff.com/robots.html

Five bomb disposal robots:
www.roboticstomorrow.com/article/2015/10/five-bomb-disposal-robots/6987/

INDEX